Painting Glass

IN A WEEKEND

Painting Glass

IN A WEEKEND

Stylish designs and practical projects

M O I R A   N E A L

A N D   L Y N D A   H O W A R T H

NEW
HOLLAND

INTRODUCTION

Decorating glassware has been a popular craft for centuries and indeed some of the glass in this book has been inspired by old Venetian work. Now that there are so many excellent products on the market, glass painting is enjoying an enormous revival and every craft magazine on the newsagents' shelves contains yet more ideas and designs.

We have inspired, supported, amused and entertained each other for almost twenty years. On many occasions our children have been reared in the inevitable chaos associated with combining our talents in creative ventures. We both became interested in glass painting when a new product, Porcelaine 150, became available which has very good dishwasher resistance and is safe to use with food — this idea really appealed and has revolutionised the craft. It means that as well as making purely decorative items or ones needing careful hand-washing, everyday glassware may be painted which will stand up to tough washing.

During the past few months we have been busy painting, stencilling, sponging, marbling and etching any and every glass item in our homes, our friends' and parents' homes. Our craving to embellish has included anything from humble jam jars and wine bottles to carafes and glasses, mirrors and even window panes ... nothing has escaped the Lynda and Moira treatment. It has led to our homes being filled with glasses no-one is allowed to drink from in case they dare drop them before this book is printed!

Trips for the weekly food shop have taken on a new appeal. Never mind what the product is, tastes like or costs — what will the bottle look like given a coat of paint? This has led to severe confusion. Just what IS that strange yellow stuff in that jam jar in the fridge? Is it mustard dressing, lemon and honey vinaigrette or custard? And how long does it keep for? If only we had labelled things before parting the mysterious contents from their beautiful containers!

And as for Jim, Lynda's husband — he became increasingly bewildered that the sponge cloth used for washing the dishes was getting smaller by the day (it was a truly marvellous discovery when we found just how good they are for sponging glassware)! All we can say is thank you Jim for putting up with us, our mess, our glass, our experiments and our masterpieces! It has certainly spared Tony, who, as anyone who has read *Dough Craft in a Weekend* will know, has a strong aversion to Moira and her mess!

We have had enormous fun putting together all the ideas in this book and we hope that you will be inspired by them. No particular artistic skill is required as we have described, step-by-step, how to arrive at the finished designs. We have provided templates and patterns where necessary but you will see from the gallery shots just how much stylish glassware can be made with just a few simple brushstrokes and dots of outliner.

Have fun!

Moira and Lynda... partners in design

GETTING STARTED

One of the greatest advantages of painting on glass is that the craft requires very little in the way of specialised tools or equipment – just a plentiful supply of new or old glassware which can be picked up for very little money. You will probably discover that much of the equipment listed below can be found around the home. This chapter explains the different paints and demonstrates the basic decorating techniques used in the projects that follow later in the book. Once you have mastered these, you will be able to create a wide range of effects and finishes and adapt them to make your own patterns.

SOURCING GLASSWARE

If, like us, you are delighted to have an excuse to go to a car boot fair or a jumble or garage sale, glass painting gives you the perfect reason! So much beautiful old glassware is available in an abundance of shapes and sizes at very reasonable prices. Even a batch of dissimilar glasses can be united into a set simply by painting them with the same colour or design motifs.

Look for unusual items such as goldfish bowls, old perfume bottles, engraved glasses, picture frames, clip frames, mirrors and vases.

Make sure you clean your glass very thoroughly before you begin painting. Really stubborn stains inside bottles may be removed with denture cleaner dissolved in hot water. Sticky labels can often be removed by rubbing with a drop of nail varnish remover on a pad of cotton wool.

EQUIPMENT AND MATERIALS

Your local hobby shop, paint outlet or mail order company will be able to supply the glass paints and other basic materials to get you started. Begin with just a few colours and add to them gradually as your skill and enthusiasm grow. The other equipment you will need to begin is listed in detail in the middle column of this page.

As soon as you have bought your glass paints you will be inspired to make a start. Do not be surprised if your first efforts look very amateurish as it can take a few projects to master this skill. It is therefore a good idea to start off with a really simple design on a jam jar in order to become familiar with the texture of the paint and its application.

It will not be long before you have exhausted your own supply of plain glass and will be requesting friends and relatives to collect empty containers for you too. Everyday packaging suddenly becomes remarkably interesting once the labels are removed and a little imagination is employed!

Interesting jars, bottles and glassware
Good quality brushes, no 2 and 4
Glass paints according to the project required. Some are solvent-based and suitable for decorative items. For more durability, choose oven-bake water-based paints
Outliner in a variety of colours
White spirit
Jam jar
Kitchen paper towels
Low-tack masking tape
Pencil
Scalpel with no 11 blade or craft knife
Tracing paper
Cocktail sticks (toothpicks)
Sponge or fur fabric
Cotton buds
Cellophane
Hairdryer
Apron
Newspaper, to protect your worksurface
Additional useful items for styling your finished work include raffia and florist's wire

TIP

To keep the mess down, once you are ready to begin, protect your workspace with layers of old newspaper or an old tablecloth as some of the paints are solvent-based and may damage some surfaces.

If children are going help with the painting, make sure they are also well covered up.

SAFETY NOTES

There is no reason why children cannot enjoy the hobby of glass painting as well as adults. Make sure that they are supervised at all times and choose water-based paints for them to use. Store paints and brush cleaner in a cool place, well out of the reach of prying hands when not in use.

Always follow manufacturers' specific instructions regarding the baking process if it is required (see facing page for more details).

A collection of glassware ready for painting

GLASS PAINTING PRODUCTS

There are many paints available on the market for painting on glass. They tend to fall into several categories:

1 Water-based paints. These do not need baking and are ideal for items which will not require washing. These are perfect for children to use too.

2 Water-based paints. These need to be baked at 200°C/400°F/gas mark 6 for 30 minutes. Items using this paint are hand-washable. The colours are bright and dense and easy to apply.

3 Porcelaine 150, Pébéo's water-based paints. These are baked at 150°C/300°F/gas mark 2. These are completely safe when in contact with food and have good dishwasher resistance. These are ideal for tableware and glasses and we have used them extensively in this book. They are available in a huge range of colours, both transparent and opaque, and once baked feel wonderfully smooth. Practice may be needed with these, as indeed with all paints, to achieve the density of cover required. It is often better to sponge on two light coats, allowing the first to dry before applying the second. There is a matt medium in the range which, if used alone, gives a wonderful, frosted effect. Used with the other colours in the range as instructed, it gives a matt finish without affecting the colour.

4 Pébéo's water-based gel paints. A new product on the market is a water-based gel which allows three-dimensional colour to be applied to glassware direct from the tube or with the aid of a palette knife. Glass nuggets, tiny mirrors and other items may then be embedded in the gel before it sets for an exotic effect. This enables you to imitate various blown glass effects, as well as creating stylish jewellery. Available in a range of colours, the gel liquifies when shaken or stirred so may also be applied with a brush.

5 Solvent-based paints. These tend to be the paints associated with the traditional stained glass look and are mainly transparent and quick drying. Replace the tops to prevent evaporation. Brushes need to be cleaned using a compatible solvent, generally white spirit. These paints are flammable and should not be used near a naked flame nor should children use them unsupervised. Make sure your work area is well ventilated.

SAFETY NOTE

Please refer to manufacturer's specific user and safety instructions regarding all glass paints. As a general rule, never paint any surface which is to come into contact with food unless the paint is non-toxic (this is why we decorated the backs of the plates) and as an extra pre-caution, avoid the lip line on glasses which are going to be functional and not simply used as decorations.

OUTLINING

The outliners used in this book are water-based, although there are some which become permanent with baking. They can be difficult to control, so practise on jam jars or cellophane before embarking on the real thing.

Have a sheet of kitchen paper ready to catch any blobs of outliner from the tube which may appear as soon as the top is removed. Start by making a row of dots and you will soon realise how little pressure is required on the tube. Progress to circles, squares, triangles and lines ①, using the practice templates on page 76. You may find you get a halo effect at times — do not worry as this

can be salvaged once the outliner has dried and can be eased back into place with the scalpel. A hairdryer is useful for speeding up the drying times of both outliners and paints but needs to be kept at least 15 cm (6 in) away from the surface to avoid damage.

USING THE GLASS PAINTS

Within about five minutes the outliner will be dry enough to apply the paint. A soft brush is essential for smooth application of the paints ①. Try filling in some of the shapes you have made with the outliners. Apply the paint with even strokes. Keep a cotton bud nearby to correct any errors and a small jar of water or solvent for brush cleaning.

SPONGING

Sponging gives a soft, delicate effect and is a very quick and easy way to apply glass paints.

Tip a few drops of the paint into a saucer (covered with cling film to reduce the cleaning up). Gently dip in your sponge pad and wipe any excess off against the edge of the dish and then test the effect on a piece of cellophane or an old jam jar before starting on your project.

One colour can be used on its own to produce a graded effect just by applying more paint onto the lowest part of the item, reducing the pressure and contact as you move up ②. A graduated effect is achieved by using several colours in succession, allowing each one to merge into the next ③.

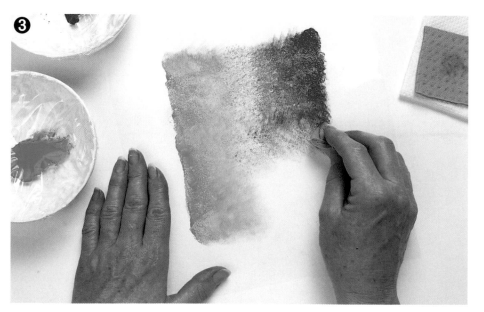

> ### TIP
>
> Thin sponge dishcloths are ideal for glass painting as they can be cut up into small pieces and discarded after use. Fine fur fabric also produces an even sponged finish but the rough edges should be folded in before use to prevent any fibres migrating onto the surface of the glass.

ETCHING

This is a very good way to add embellishment without having to [use?] another colour. It is perfect for a[dding] details like feathers, scales on fish and so on as well as creating abst[ract] designs on a sponged surface. You need to etch the design as soon a[s the] paint has been applied and there [are] several ways of doing it. Use a co[cktail] stick or toothpick for very fine d[etail] or for details on tiny items. A typ[ical] 'pencil' type of rubber is ideal for chunkier etching and may be sha[ped] with a knife or pencil sharpener depending on the effect required. Knitting needles work well too.

Sponged and etched snowflake p[late]

SPONGE DOT APPLICATORS

A really simple way to apply uniform dots to a project is to make your own applicators. Peel a foam dishcloth into two and then cut it into 2 cm (¾ in) squares. Bind each one over the end of a cocktail stick or toothpick using fuse wire. Make several as you will find them a useful addition to your equipment kit!

STENCILLING

This is a good way to decorate glassware with a regular repeat pattern. It is particularly useful if you intend to sell your finished items as it is very quick to do once the initial stencil cutting has been done.

To make your stencils, photocopy the required template (see page 77), use adhesive mount to attach it to the card you are using and allow the glue to dry for about ten minutes before attempting to cut it. Protect your worksurface with a cutting mat, cork mat or a thick layer of newspaper before you start. Use a metal ruler as a guide for cutting straight lines ①. Avoid trying to cut around angular designs in one go; instead, make several shorter cuts ②.

It is worth taking care in order to get good, professional results and the initial investment in a craft knife or scalpel and plenty of spare blades is worthwhile. For one-off stencils to decorate flat surfaces, thin card is ideal or even a good quality paper. If you are using your stencil on a curved surface, you may need to use either thin paper or specialist adhesive stencilling film which moulds more easily to the contours of the glass.

USING STENCILS

Lightly spray the back of the stencil with aerosol glue and press it onto the object to be decorated. On cylindrical items you may also need to secure the stencil with a couple of rubber bands.

③ Pour a little glass paint into a saucer and use either a piece of old

4

Simple, Shaker-style stenc

sponge or fur fabric to
It is always worth exp
stage and we found th
wonderfully well for a
texture. Sponge will g
even texture which is
rustic style projects ④

MASKING AND
STENCILLING

Many different object
mask out clear areas
you decorate with sp
marbling. Stick on sh
hearts, flowers, initia

ETCHING

This is a very good way to add embellishment without having to use another colour. It is perfect for adding details like feathers, scales on fish, eyes and so on as well as creating abstract designs on a sponged surface. You will need to etch the design as soon as the paint has been applied and there are several ways of doing it. Use a cocktail stick or toothpick for very fine designs or for details on tiny items. A typist's 'pencil' type of rubber is ideal for chunkier etching and may be sharpened with a knife or pencil sharpener depending on the effect required ①. Knitting needles work well too.

MARBLING

A wonderful range of patterns may be produced using this technique which involves floating coloured solvent-based glass paints on a suitable medium. We have kept the procedure simple and have avoided the use of specialist marbling mediums in preference for water and wallpaper paste. You will need to use a bowl larger than the size of the item to be marbled and cover the worksurface with plenty of paper before you begin.

Two of the projects in this book have marbling as one of the stages of producing the final item. Refer to pages 22 and 58 for fuller instructions.

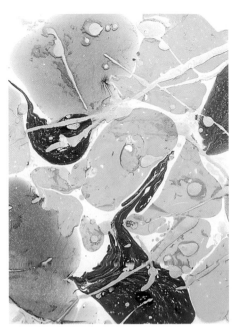

Sponged and etched snowflake plate

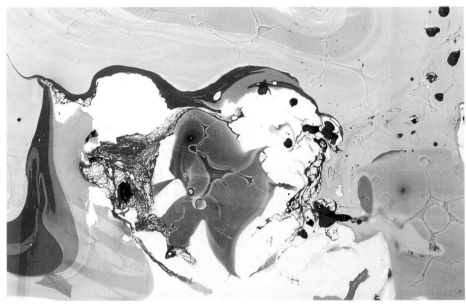

An exotic effect created by marbling a simple piece of glass

TRANSFERRING DESIGNS

The easiest way to transfer a design onto glass is to trace it. Tape the design to the inside or back of the object to hold it firmly against the glass. If the surface is curved, make many small vertical slits to enable the pattern to conform to the glass. Trace over the pattern with outliner.

NARROW NECKED BOTTLES

It is impossible to tape the design to the inside of narrow necked bottles but there is a simple solution. Make sure the bottle is dry inside and then, on a piece of paper, cut out the design to the height of the bottle. Roll up the paper, push it into the bottle, then pour in pasta or lentils right up to the top and the design is perfectly anchored! ①

❷

❶

EMBELLISHMENTS

The addition of those lovely shiny glass nuggets available in a myriad of colours gives a very splendid finish to an otherwise ordinary item. Tiny rhinestones and sequins may be used too and they are available from craft shops or mail order companies ②.

Apply them to your glassware before the paint using a specialist glass glue to

REVERSE PAINTING TECHNIQUE

This is a very handy way to decorate the back of a glass plate so that the cutting surface will not become

damaged when the plate is used. It is also useful if you wish to use paints which are not safe when in contact with food. A little planning is needed before you begin because the details, normally left until last, must be painted on first. Just think in reverse and remember to reverse any text too!

These iridescent nuggets inspired this floral design

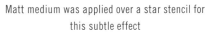

Matt medium was applied over a star stencil for this subtle effect

ensure good adhesion. If you are giving a filled, decorated bottle to a friend as a present, spend some time adding a label, a pretty stopper or sealing wax. See our gallery pages for more ideas. Remember, a beautifully presented item will quickly lead to orders if you want to sell your glassware.

INSPIRATION FOR DESIGNS

Wrapping paper, gift cards, colouring books, curtain fabrics, flower and bulb catalogues are good sources of inspiration. Do remember, however, that you may not sell any work using other people's designs.

For a baby gift you could use the nursery wallpaper design to inspire the edge of a mirror or picture frame. Glasses, jugs and carafes decorated to match existing crockery or table linen make excellent gifts for adults and may be themed to celebrate a special occasion, such as a milestone birthday or anniversary.

If you enjoy museums, why not visit one and get inspiration from old

Venetian glassware? We found some fascinating pieces where much of the design is made up of dots and swirls — very easy to reproduce as you will see from our Historical Gallery on page 30.

This design was adapted from traditional East European glassware

PROJECTS AND GALLERIES
FOR PAINTING GLASS

GOLDFISH PLATE

A shoal of golden fish swim around this plate which is both practical and attractive. You could use it to brighten up your bathroom, and could decorate other items such as a soap dish or toothbrush mug to match. As the plate is decorated on the underside, it may be used for serving food.

1 Wash the plate in hot soapy water and dry carefully. Start by sponging the edge of the plate on the underside with the gold paint, applying it densely around the outside. Allow the paint to look feathery on the inner edge. Use the paper towel and white spirit to clean any paint from the front of the plate.

YOU WILL NEED

A glass plate
Solvent-based glass paints in gold and white
Fine sponge or fur fabric
White spirit
Kitchen paper towels
No 2 paintbrush
Cellophane to practise on
Kitchen paper towels
Fish and surf templates (page 70)
Sticky tape
Paper
Pen
Scissors
Cocktail stick (toothpick)
Aerosol spray mount
Saucer covered with cling film

— VARIATIONS —

This plate could be painted using oven-bake paints if you want to preserve the pattern during frequent use. It seems a pity to hide it away in a cupboard when not in use, so why not store it on a plate display stand?

2 Copy the large fish template and tape it to the inside of the plate, positioning it centrally. Working on the back of the plate, paint the fish gold, but do not apply the markings at this stage.

3 Remove the template and use it as a guide to etch in the details of the scales and gills using the cocktail stick. Keep the tip clean with the paper towel.

4 Paint the shoal of tiny goldfish next. This time have a practise run on cellophane first as it is easier to copy the tiny shapes we have given you. Use the cocktail stick to etch in the details after every third or fourth fish. For a bit of fun, paint one little fish swimming the wrong way! Allow the plate to dry for about an hour while you make the surf template for the next stage.

5 Draw around the plate onto a piece of paper. Cut out the circle and then fold it in half four times to make 16 equal sections. Open it out flat and mark 1 cm (½ in) in from the edge all the way round. Trace the surf template onto each marked section. Pour some of the white paint onto the saucer, dip the sponge into it and wipe the excess off on the edge. Sponge the surf design all around the plate. Remove the template and quickly soften the edges of the wave design by carefully sponging over it. Turn the plate over every now and then to check what it looks like from the front. Leave the plate upside down to dry for 24 hours before use.

OLIVE OIL BOTTLES

This project would make an ideal present. After painting the the olives and leaves on the glass, we filled the bottles with finest quality olive oil and attached a small pastry brush by drilling through the handle and attaching a length of wire. Choose a brush which is slightly shorter than the bottle.

1 First, wash and dry the bottle thoroughly inside and out. Trace or photocopy the template and cut it out close to the edge of the design. Tape a piece of ribbon or string to the top for easy removal from narrow necked bottles. Push the template into the bottle. Fill the bottle with pasta to anchor the paper in place and then stopper it firmly.

YOU WILL NEED

A tall bottle (ours is 27 cm (11 in) tall) with a cork stopper	Solvent-based glass paints in brown, emerald green, yellow, red and blue
Template (page 70)	Saucer covered with cling film for mixing colours
Paper	White spirit
Pen	Cocktail stick (toothpick)
Scissors	Kitchen paper towel
Sticky tape	Wooden pastry brush (optional)
Ribbon or string	Drill (optional)
Pasta, baking beans or similar	Florist's wire (optional)
No 2 paintbrush	

VARIATIONS

This bottle would make a lovely gift for anyone to display in their kitchen. Use this idea for salad dressings too. Artistically minded people will have fun decorating bottles of flavoured oil or vinegar with sprays of chillies or a variety of herbs.

2 Start by painting the olive branches using the brown paint darkened with a little blue if necessary. You may find it easier to rest your hand on something of similar height (we found a paper towel roll works very well as a cushion to steady the wrist).

3 You need to mix emerald green with a little brown and yellow to achieve the leaf shade we have used. Test the colour on cellophane but remember it does not have to be botanically correct! Paint in the leaves using the illustration as a guide. Use the white spirit to keep your brush clean and to remove mistakes.

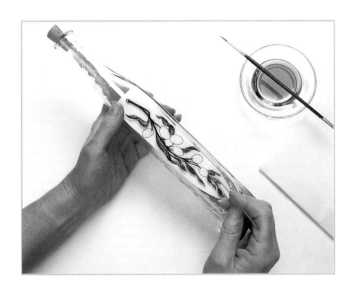

4 Etch in the details of the leaves using a cocktail stick. It is best to do this as soon as possible before the paint has time to dry. This technique really does bring the leaves to life. Alternatively, paint in the veins using a darker shade of green.

5 Finally, paint in the olives using a mixture of red, blue and brown. If you are happy with your work, allow it to dry thoroughly. If not, remove it and start again! To give the bottle a rustic appearance, add a hook made from wire which is then twisted around the neck of the bottle. Fill the bottle with extra virgin olive oil and then firmly wire the cork stopper in place.

YELLOW GALLERY

'Volcano' oil burner
This has been etched and over-painted.

Tall yellow bottle
This elegant bottle has been stencil-frosted for a pretty finish.

Orange slices jar
A citrus effect was achieved by applying the paint with a very small brush and fine brushstrokes.

Shallow yellow platter
A very simple gold border was painted around this dish for a striking effect.

Cup and saucer
Luscious apricots were painted on this cup using opaque glass paints.

Shaped glasses
One glass has been painted with simple bands of yellow and gold and the other given an iridescent effect by being lightly sponged first with gold and then with a clear yellow. A simple band of gold dots was added later.

1940s' style glass dessert dish

Bottom: The embossed lines on this dish made it very simple to decorate with yellows, orange and gold.

Tall, pale yellow glass

The bowl of this glass was made from pale lemon glass but a deeper colour was overlaid using clear yellow paint.

Stripy frosted glass

Strips of paper were used to mask off areas and matt medium then sponged on to give a frosted look.

Perfume bottle

Matt medium was used on this little bottle first and then the yellow paint applied, making the glass appear transparent again.

Hexagonal jar

Bottom: Low-tack tape was used to mask off alternate facets before marbling with yellow, orange and gold. Gold outliner dots were added later.

Copper glass

This glass was frosted with matt medium first before a coat of copper was sponged over the bottom section.

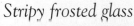

MILLEFIORI LANTERN

This lantern was inspired by the wonderful range of colours found in millefiori beads. It is surprisingly easy to reproduce the design but can only be successfully done on a flat surface. As the panels of this lantern are removable, it is ideal for decorating in this way and candlelight enhances the rich colours.

1 Clean the panels of glass using glass cleaner, being very careful of the sharp edges. (Wear the leather gloves for protection.) Lay your glass onto a sheet of paper and draw round it and then use small coins as templates as shown. If you prefer, use the template on page 71.

VARIATIONS

Faceted bottles and jam jars may be decorated using this method but make sure that your chosen item is kept completely level at all times until baked.

2 Lay the panel of glass onto the pattern and remove the lids from all the tubes of outliners before you begin. It is best to work on just three circles at a time and vary the colour combinations using an equal amount of colour overall. Begin with the red. The fluid nature of the outliners make them ideal for this project.

3 Continue to add more colours in circles and dots in an effort to achieve a star or floral effect. Note how well the colours look juxtaposed to the nearest colour in the rainbow, i.e. red, orange, yellow, green and blue. This stops complementary colours (e.g. orange and blue) merging and becoming sludgy within each 'bead'. Aim to use all the colours on each one and do not worry if your work looks blobby at this stage.

4 Once you have completed three of the 'beads', use the cocktail stick to start the feathering. Drag the colours in and out all the way round each one to create a spider's web effect and encourage the colours to blend and bleed into one another.

5 Continue to work down the panel of glass towards yourself to avoid smudging your work. The paint looks very dense and opaque at this stage until it is thoroughly dry. When you have finished the panel, set it aside and start the next one. Note how all the colours continue to bleed into each other. This will continue to happen as the panels are left to dry flat for at least the next 24 hours. Bake following the manufacturer's instructions. Allow to cool and then fill in the spaces with solvent-based glass paint if you wish. Leave to dry thoroughly before reassembling the lantern.

RUBY AND GOLD SUNDAE DISHES

The inspiration for this design comes from Middle Eastern tea glasses and if you are able to find any plain glasses, the design may be adapted to suit them.

If you are feeling adventurous, why not make a complete dinner service using this design?

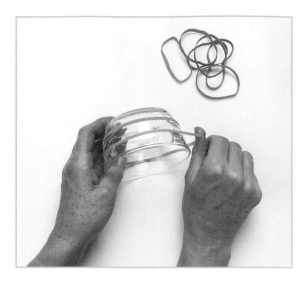

1 Wash the glassware in hot soapy water, rinse and dry thoroughly. Cover your work area with paper before you begin. Use the rubber bands to mask off a parallel strip around the dish. The width may be varied depending on the size of your dish, but be sure to make them all equidistant.

VARIATIONS

The dishes could each be painted in a different colour as long as each is strong enough to contrast with the gold. Practise first before going on to the real thing. The central band would make an attractive decoration on wine glasses too.

2 Fill the masked off area with the ruby paint, keeping the bowl clear of the work top to avoid smudging. Keep a paper towel to hand for brush cleaning before moving on to the next step.

3 The narrow gold bands are added next, along with the wavy gold line which forms the basis for the leaf and tendril design. Have a practice run on cellophane first using the template (see page 70) as a guide.

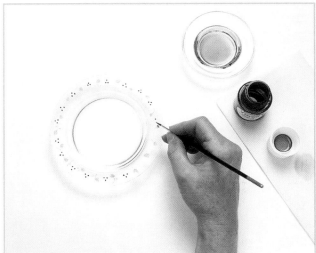

4 Once you are confident painting the leaf and tendril design, paint them on the bowls. If your artistic ability is not up to it, try painting little groups of three dots or simple tendrils instead.

5 Finally, work on the saucers. The leaf design is echoed around the edge in gold, followed by groups of three red dots in between.

HISTORICAL GALLERY

Spotted 1950s' style glass

Bottom: Use a fine brush to apply spots in a variety of colours.

Miniature perfume bottles

These little bottles are surprisingly cheap to buy and very quickly decorated with simple brushstrokes and outliner.

Old jam pot

The engraved design on this delightful old jam pot has been highlighted with gold, with fuschias delicately painted around the top.

Hexagonal jar

Bottom: Simple brushstrokes were used for the flowers and gold and white leaf shapes decorate the edges.

Venetian-style bottle

The simple brushstrokes on the edges of this bottle were inspired by old Venetian glassware. The lady was painted first with an opaque white and then the green and red clear paints applied on top.

Art Deco bottle

Simple lines and clean colours inspired by the Art Deco movement.

Champagne glass

Bottom: Red and green were drizzled down this old fashioned champagne glass and dots of colour added too.

Recycled perfume bottle

This beautiful lady in her crinoline dress is definitely for the more artistic reader!

Heraldic goblet

This is a good example of allowing the shape of the glass dictate the style of the embellishment. Here, the design has been added in black, white and gold.

Thistle glass

Bottom: This engraved bargain buy has been transformed with the use of colour.

Hexagonal boxes

Simple Art Nouveau motifs have been applied in gold and black.

ANTIQUED ETRUSCAN-STYLE VASE

The little stoppered jug used for this project started life filled with salad dressing which has now become one of the anonymous substances in the fridge! The idea can be adapted to any bottle or jug you can find either hiding at the back of your cupboard or on your next trip to the supermarket. Several pieces may be decorated in a similar way to make an interesting and original display.

1 Sponge the top half of the vase with the green paint allowing it to fade around the middle. The sponging can look quite rough as you are aiming for an aged look. Leave for a few minutes to dry between this and the next three steps.

4 Highlight the edges of the vase with the gold, including the rim and handle. The idea is to make the worn surfaces look metallic.

YOU WILL NEED

Glass jug (ours was filled with salad dressing which is now in a jam jar!)	No 2 paintbrush
	Kitchen paper towels
Oven-bake paints such as Porcelaine 150 in pale green, slate blue, pewter and gold	Pewter outliner
	Fine sponge
Matt medium	Domestic oven

2 Using the blue paint, sponge from the bottom upwards and over the first coat. Allow the paint to fade out as you work upwards.

3 Antique over the base of the jug with the pewter, adding light touches of the metallic colour to the neck of the jug and the handle. Again, precision is unimportant as a rough look is more authentic.

5 Paint swirls of matt medium at random on the vase. The paint looks milky when it is applied but dries to a very subtle finish.

6 Echo the swirls using the pewter outliner. This dries to give an extra dimension to the vase. Leave the vase to dry for 24 hours before baking following manufacturer's instructions.

VARIATIONS

Try making a collection of glassware using this technique. Similar glassware is readily available and very quick to decorate in this way and several pieces could be painted at the same time.

FIFTIES STYLE CARAFE AND TUMBLERS

This really is a 20-minute project! It is brilliantly easy to do and as the shapes are so simple, they require no artistic ability – if you can write, you can reproduce them once you have mastered using the paints.

1 Copy the template on page 71 and lay the cellophane over it in order to have a practice run if you are not sufficiently confident to start straight onto the glassware. Keep a sheet of paper towel to hand and use it to keep the nozzle clean before drawing each motif. Apply the paints sparingly as they will spread slightly over the next ten minutes.

VARIATIONS

Why not decorate the backs of glass plates and bowls to make a complete table setting?

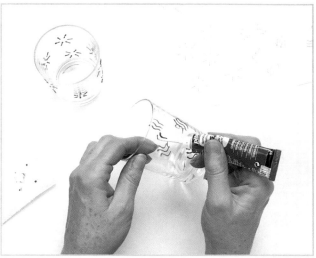

2 Once you are ready to start on the glasses, wash them with hot, soapy water. The black squiggles are fun to do and it is best to do these freehand in order to get a flowing line. The black diamond design is easiest to work in two stages, working from the top to the bottom of one side and then the next.

3 Magenta sunbursts are worked from the outside inwards, making up the six spokes. The second magenta design of three wavy lines is then worked on the next glass.

4 The green triangular design is worked next and then the green dot design. Finally, transfer all the designs to the carafe, starting with the black, followed by the magenta and then the green. The groups of three dots can be added last of all as they are small and make good 'fillers'.

5 Leave all the glassware to dry for 24 hours and then use the scalpel to ease any stray outliner gently into place before baking following the manufacturer's instructions. Wash the glassware before use.

SUNFLOWER PLATE

This moulded plate lends itself to being painted as a sunflower. If you are unable to buy a similar one, the design could be applied to the back of a plain plate if you make a simple template first by folding a circle of paper into equal segments. Draw a circle for the centre of the flower and then stick the template onto the inside of the plate before you begin.

1 Lightly brush the petals and centre of the design with the gold. Use it sparingly so that the other colours, to be applied later, will shine through. Set aside to dry.

2 It is time to experiment now while the gold paint dries. Use a piece of cellophane to work out the colour density you want to achieve before working on the plate. Use delicate brush strokes.

3 Use the palest shade of yellow first and brush it evenly, following the direction of the petals. Work the second yellow over it, working about two-thirds of the way up the petals so that the outer edges are paler.

4 Use the orange to darken from the centre of each petal to about half way down, using the brush almost dry to give a light, feathery look.

5 The centre of the sunflower is stippled using a mixture of brown, black and orange to give the appearance of seeds. Leave the plate to dry for 24 hours before baking according to the manufacturer's instructions. It may then be used and washed frequently without damage.

BLACK, SILVER AND GOLD GALLERY

Etched cork-stoppered jar
Bottom: This jar was frosted with matt medium with the design etched out afterwards.

Oak and acorn glass
Bottom: This design was stencilled on and the detail etched out with a cocktail stick.

Jug
Bottom: As simple as ABC! Letters were drawn on the jug and black dots added around the top.

Black plate
These stunning white brushstrokes look very oriental but are, in fact, simple random strokes.

Cocktail glass
Two coats of gold on the outside of this glass were followed by random black spots for a stylish finish.

Marbled plate
Here black, white and gold paints were floated on water and the design picked up on the back of the plate.

Frosted carafe
Oak leaves have been stencilled on this carafe using matt medium.

Art Deco jar

Bottom: This jar has been decorated very simply with stylised deer.

Glasses

Below: It is so easy to unite several dissimilar glasses like these with a common colour scheme. Black, gold and white paints and outliners were used to apply the designs.

Christmas bauble

Not even the humble bauble can escape decoration! This one was patterned with outliner.

Art Deco perfume bottle

Centre: This bottle was sponged with silver and gold before the stylised design was added in black.

Black and white dappled plate

Blobs of black and white paint were dropped onto the back of the plate and then spread and etched with a cocktail stick.

Perfume bottle

Bottom: This bottle embellished with trefoils was decorated in the same way as the project on page 48.

Gold and black glass

This glass was made in the same way as the set of decorated glasses with bands on page 28.

PERFUME BOTTLE

Have you ever thought what a pity it is to throw out your empty perfume bottles, especially when they are often such lovely shapes? Here is the answer. The design can be applied to any size or shape of bottle and a group of dissimilar bottles can be united in this way to make an attractive collection for the bedroom or bathroom.

1 Wash and dry the bottle thoroughly before you begin. Cover the entire surface by sponging it with the pewter paint. Apply two or three light coats, allowing the paint to dry between coats. In this way you will build up a really deep, lustrous surface. Allow to dry for 24 hours and bake following manufacturer's instructions. This will make a much better surface to work on and mistakes can be easily removed.

YOU WILL NEED

Small decorative bottle or empty perfume bottle

Oven-bake glass paints such as Porcelaine 150 in pewter, black and ivory

Fine sponge

Trefoil pattern (page 72)

Cellophane for practice runs

No 2 paintbrush

Water

Kitchen paper towels

Domestic oven

2 It is a good idea at this stage to have a practice run at painting the trefoils. To copy the pattern, lay cellophane over the template and paint as many as you need using one colour until you feel sufficiently confident to paint them freehand.

3 Check the spacing of the trefoils by laying the cellophane over your chosen bottle. This will give you an idea of how and where to place the shapes.

4 Now you are ready to start on the bottle. Paint all the ivory shapes in first, remembering to leave room for the other two colours.

5 Paint the black trefoils next and then fill in the gaps with a silvery mix of black and pewter. Leave to dry for a further 24 hours and bake again.

FLORAL ROUNDELS

These roundels make a refreshing change from the usual stained glass versions that are now seen everywhere. They are a perfect way to brighten up a window and look attractive when the sunlight shines through them.

1 If your roundel is not the same size as ours, use a photocopier to enlarge or reduce the template to the required dimmensions. Lay the template on the worksurface and tape the roundel over it, being careful to position the tape over plain areas of the pattern.

YOU WILL NEED

Glass roundel — ours is 13 cm (5 in)

Template (page 74)

Masking tape

Black outliner

Craft knife or scalpel

No 2 paintbrush

Solvent-based paints such as Vitrail in ruby and chartreuse

Cellophane for practice runs

White spirit

Kitchen paper towels

Hairdryer (optional)

VARIATIONS

These designs could be used as jam pot covers if the designs were worked on cellophane using black paint instead of outliner. Enlarge or reduce the design according to the size of the jar and use white tissue underneath it to show off the design.

2 With the outliner, carefully follow the outlines of the flowers and leaves using steady, even pressure. Start at the top and work towards yourself to avoid smudging. Keep a paper towel to hand to remove any blobs of outliner from the tip of the nozzle. Leave to dry or speed up the process with the hairdryer.

3 If there are any imperfections in the outlining they can be salvaged at this stage. Use a scalpel to scratch off any rough areas and use the paintbrush to gently brush loosened outliner away from the surface.

4 Practise your brush strokes on cellophane using the ruby paint. Once you are confident, start working on the flowers and brush the petals from the centre outwards to obtain light, feathery strokes.

5 Finally, paint the leaves with the green paint varying the density of the paint for a more realistic effect and to build up depth.

TURQUOISE GALLERY

Stoppered bottle

White lilies have been painted on this bottle with silver used for the stamens. Look through flower catalogues for similar ideas.

Tall turquoise vase

Gold outliner has been applied to give a 'punched' look in simple spirals and curves.

Floral jar

Bottom: Green and silver paints were used to brighten up this jam jar. A little white was added to the silver for the outer parts of the petals and the white dots of paint applied last.

Goldfish jar

Below: This would be fun to fill with bubble bath as a gift for a child. The fish were painted with outliner first and then with a coat of clear yellow glass paint.

Fish platter

Gold was lightly brushed on the back of this plate and then a variety of blues, greens and turquoises painted over it.

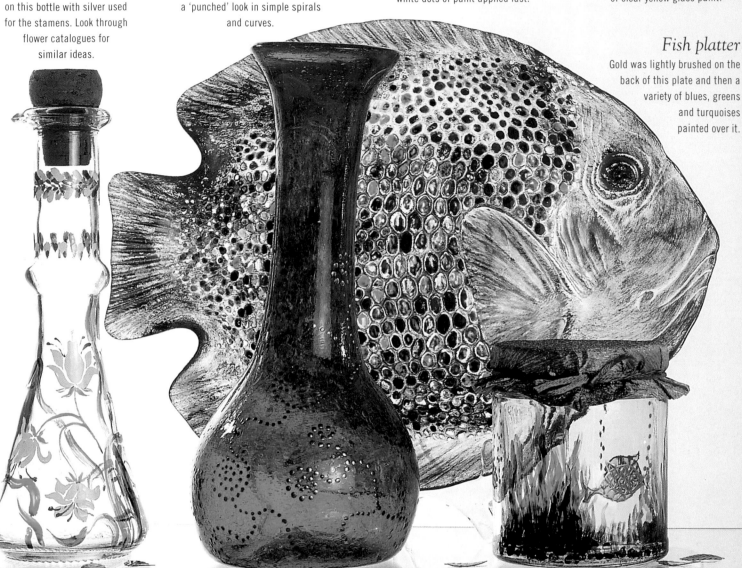

Two-tone glass
Bottom: Transparent oven-bake paints in green and blue were sponged onto this little glass to give a graduated effect.

Marbled plate
The edge of the plate was painted with gold and allowed to dry before turquoise, green, purple and gold paints were floated on water, and the plate marbled with them.

Cup and saucer
Below: Just imagine sipping fruit tea from this cup, beautifully painted with blackcurrants. Why not make a set featuring a variety of fruits?

Multi-faceted jug
This old jug was picked up at a junk shop and transformed by being sponged with a range of oven-bake paints. Pewter outliner was then dotted around each colour.

Tall vase
Simple brushstrokes in shades of blues, greens and gold make this a very quick and easy project.

Turquoise tumbler
Left: The black lines were applied first and then green, white and gold paints to fill some of the spaces.

Clip frame
Black outliner was allowed to trail in wiggly lines around the frame. Once it was dry, some of the spaces were filled with green, gold and purple paints.

Encrusted bottle
Chunky glass nuggets were first glued in place on this bottle and the design worked around them.

RED GALLERY

Sundae dish

Below: The top part of the dish was sponged with red, while gold was used for the lower part. Once dry, tiny spots of gold outliner were added as a decorative pattern.

Fleur de lys jar

Bottom left: Flat-sided jam jars are ideal for decorating. This one was sponged first and then the design added with gold outliner.

Triangular red bottle

Bottom: Sponging forms the basis of the pattern on both these bottles. Outliner has been used for the relief patterns.

Valentine platter

Simple and sweet for the one you love!

Faceted jar

This design was inspired by old glassware and could be used very effectively in a range of colours on a set of sundae dishes or tumblers.

Octagonal dish

Positive and negative stencilling has been used to decorate this dish with heart motifs.

Heart-shaped crown bottle

Bottom: Coloured glass bottles are widely available and are easy to decorate. This one features simple but effective designs.

Bow glass

The bottom part of this glass was sponged with gold. Once dry, the bow motif was stencilled on. You could cut your own stencil or use a commercial one.

Strawberry cup

Bottom: You do need some artistic skill to reproduce this design, but it could be simplified or even stencilled. Why not paint a set of glass cups with a selection of fruits and use them to serve fruit teas?

Faceted jug

This wonderful old jug was found at a local junk shop. It lends itself to this kind of decoration and similar pieces of glass are easy to find. A combination of painting and relief work has been used.

Spotty bottle

Mineral drinks come in a superb range of shapes and sizes and are ideal for revamping and re-using.

CHRISTMAS PLATTER

It seems a pity to cover the design on this Christmas plate but it is perfect for serving up hot mince pies on a wintry day. The pattern is on the back, making a series of these plates ideal as special dinner plates if they are washed with care. Christmas trees or ivy leaves could be substituted for holly.

1 Make the reverse stencil for the gold edging by folding a piece of paper in half and then into quarters. Fold in half diagonally twice so that you have 16 layers of paper with the fold lines radiating out from the central point. Use the ruler to measure the radius of the flat base of the plate, and then mark this measurement on the paper from the central point outwards. Cut the 'V' shape as shown in the photograph. Open out the paper (you should have a circle with a pointed edge) and lightly spray with aerosol mount. Leave for a few seconds and then stick to the back of the plate.

VARIATIONS

Why not make a complete set of Christmas glasses to match the plate? The holly design could be reduced on a photocopier and the holly and berries painted around the glass bowl. Sponge gold on the base, stem and bottom of the bowl.

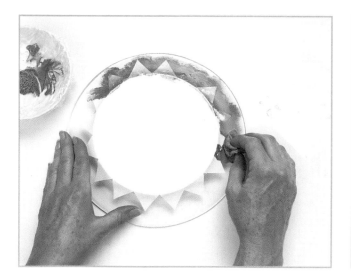

2 Pour a little of the gold paint into the saucer and then sponge over the edge of the template all the way round. Apply the paint densely at the edge of the template to give a sharp outline and less densely near the rim of the plate. Remove the template and leave to dry.

3 Meanwhile, cut the holly stencils using the holly patterns given on page 76. As the points of the leaves are very fine, it is worth using a new scalpel blade before attempting to cut them. Cut out the stars too. Use a cutting mat to protect the worksurface and leave a border of about 1 cm (½ in) around each one. Lightly spray the backs with the aerosol adhesive.

4 Stencil the gold stars in the centre and allow them to dry. Mix the green paints to achieve the desired colour and then stencil about three leaves around the base of the plate using the sponge. Use the photo as a guide and vary the angle of the leaves as you go. We have given you three different leaf sizes to make it look more interesting. Use the cocktail stick to etch in the veining details of each leaf before stencilling the next three.

5 Use the paintbrush to fill in the gaps with the holly berries. We have mixed a rich ruby red colour for them. Leave to dry thoroughly before using.

TEMPLATES

The templates shown here are actual size.
They may be easily enlarged or reduced on a
photocopier to suit the size of the glass to
be decorated.

Goldfish plate
Large and small fish,
centre fish and wave motif
(see page 18)

Olive oil bottle
Olive spray (see page 20)

Ruby and gold sundae dishes
Leaf and tendril design (see page 28)

Millefiori lantern
(see page 26)

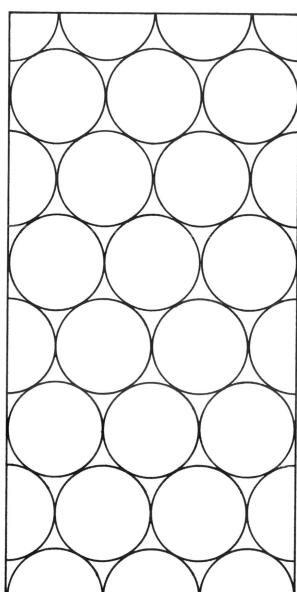

Tasselled champagne glasses
Rope and tassels (see page 38)

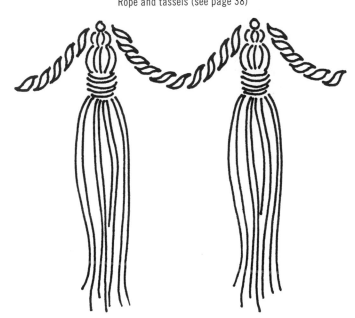

Fifties-style carafe and tumblers
Six different motifs (see page 34)

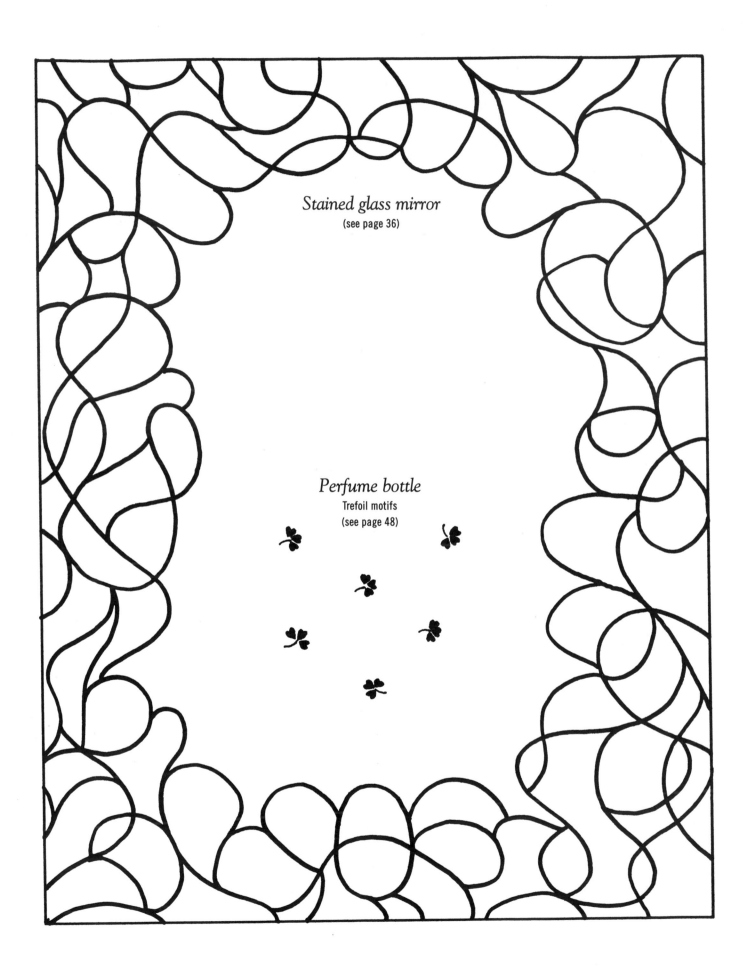

Stained glass mirror
(see page 36)

Perfume bottle
Trefoil motifs
(see page 48)

Frosted glass window
Cockerel, heart and blocks pattern
for stencil making
(see page 52)

Starry oil burner
Star shapes (see page 44)

INDEX